HOW NOT TO TREK
TO MOUNT EVEREST

HOW NOT TO TREK
TO MOUNT EVEREST

*A TRUE STORY ABOUT TREKKING TO EVEREST BASE CAMP WITH
NO PLANNING, NO SLEEPING BAG AND HAVING TO RUN BACK
DOWN DUE TO BEING LATE FOR A WEDDING*

By Cory McLeod

SDS

AN 'SDS PUBLISHING' PAPERBACK

© Copyright 2020
Cory McLeod

A CIP catalogue record for this title is
available from the British Library.

ISBN 978 1 7109649 2 9

SDS Publishing
7 Woodpark Avenue
Knaresborough
HG5 9DJ
Email : davidcayre@ntlworld.com
Website : www.david-c-ayre.co.uk

CONTENTS

HOW NOT TO TREK
TO MOUNT EVEREST

Who – on Earth, am I?

"As you travel solo, being totally responsible for yourself, it's inevitable that you will discover just how capable you are."

Not very, as you're about to find out.

My name is Cory McLeod and I am originally from Harrogate, a small town in the north of England. My friends and family say I've lived just about as interesting life as a normal person with limited funds can. Whether it be driving the length of India in a tuk-tuk, being held at gun point in South America or climbing Mount Fuji with a broken rib, I try to make life as difficult and exciting as possible.

Full speed ahead,   **Halfway up Mount**
Rickshaw Run   **Fuji**

Aside from travelling, my father – Ian, produced a film on YouTube that went viral around the world. He took a photo of me every day of my life from birth to aged 21 and made it into a time-lapse film called *21 Years*. The idea for the project which Ian was quoted as saying "I had over a few glasses of wine," reached over 6.5 million views and had us doing interviews all over the world.

Me and Dad at The Louvre

21 Years YouTube video

I am still taking the photos and plan to release the next video on my 30th birthday in September 2021. It's been great to continue the project whilst I have been travelling, as it has allowed me to take photos in some really cool locations.

I think my first taste for travelling came from being 15 months old when my parents took me backpacking around Chile in South America for three months. Strapped tight on to my dad's chest we travelled the full length of the country, ending up in Torres del Paine and Punta Arenas, Patagonia. Whilst I don't remember the trip of course, the photos and stories were always shared and spoken about and I've always taken great pride in my parents taking me on a journey like that at such a young age.

Found a local friend, Punta Arenas

Exploring Patagonia with Mum

Growing up in school I was always fascinated learning about new countries and cultures. Apart from learning about soil formation and erosion I used to have a real passion for Geography as I could impress about my knowledge and understanding of many places around the world.

Oatlands Junior School,

From an early age I knew as soon as I finished school, I wanted to see the world and visit as many countries as possible, so by age 17 in my final year I started to plan my gap year.

My father was born in Antofagasta, Chile in 1956 to my grandparents Cecilia and Ronald. Ronald was living in Paraguay and Argentina as a child, but in 1942 when he became of age, he boarded the *Highland Princess* ship to the U.K. to volunteer for the Royal Air Force, during the Second World War. By chance, when he was sent on a post, he met Cecilia in Scotland, who was previously living in Chile. After noticing his uniform at a ballroom dance, Cecilia addressed him by saying "Hola Argentino." From that day on, they met regularly during the evenings and weekends and started to write to each other every day.

Grandad Ronnie said "It was the luckiest and most wonderful meeting of my whole life!" They got married during the war and then moved back to South America in

1946. Some years later, they had Ian and both his sisters Elisabeth and Margaret, before moving them to the U.K. to try and gain a better education. Elisabeth eventually moved back to Chile with my grandparents, whilst Margaret and Ian stayed in the U.K.

With such a heavy South American influence, I decided this would be the best place to start on what would be the first of many journeys. With my two friends Richard and Tom, we embarked on a backpacking trip of a lifetime that would take us through Chile, Brazil, Argentina, Bolivia and Peru. Some of the most noteworthy experiences included climbing up to Machu Picchu, one of the *Seven Wonders of the World*, cycling 'Death Road' in Bolivia (the most dangerous road in the world) and camping in the Atacama Desert.

Cecilia and Ronnie

Overlooking Machu Picchu

Cycling 'Death Road' in Bolivia

Football at Salar de Atacama

After this trip I was hooked by the backpacking lifestyle and it saw me travel to countries such as Indonesia, Thailand, Sri Lanka, Maldives and India. However, there was always one goal, a dream of mine my entire life – to see Mount Everest. I'm not even sure where this dream originated. Maybe it was from watching films or documentaries as a kid, but I always felt captivated and charmed by the sheer scale of it.

Koh Phi Phi viewpoint, Thailand

Gili Islands, Indonesia   **Maldives on a budget**

Sigiriya Rock, Sri Lanka

Monkey chilling in Dambulla

I knew I would go at some point; I just didn't know when and under what circumstances. In all my life dreaming about it I never thought it would happen like it did.

How It All Started

To set it up for you, basically I was in Sydney, May 2017 on a working holiday. After years of missing family events I was forced to fly back for my cousins wedding. I wanted to be there; it's just it wasn't too convenient when I lived on the other side of the world. It was the first wedding out of all of the cousin's and apparently, I had promised to be there. Of course, they didn't chip in for the one thousand, two hundred and fifty-five-pound flight. Fortunately, this trip tied in with a muddy little festival called Glastonbury which I managed to get a ticket for, so this softened the blow.

There was absolutely no chance I was flying all the way back from near Antarctica in one go, so I started to look up different ways and routes of getting back to the U.K. I pulled up a map and looked at flights going right or left, or east or west, or whatever you call it. At the time, I was working seven days a week at Watsons Bay Boutique Hotel in Sydney

12

– a really fun beach bar, with around one hundred like-minded staff members.

Sunset view, Watsons Bay

Watsons with Lauren, Kate and Manda

Having fun with workmates Matteo, Dan and Mel

Good times with work colleagues Matteo, Dan and Mel

Honestly, if you've not been to Australia – go! It's not just England in the sun. It's a million times better. Everyone is so laid back; the weather is unbelievable and especially in a place like Sydney there are people living there from all over the world. At work we had staff from Mexico, Brazil, Spain, Sweden and Canada - it puts a smile on my face just thinking about it. We would all smash work out and then get smashed ourselves afterwards. Same every day, on repeat.

The first person I met at work was Gabriela from São Paulo. We were working behind the bar and I think she could tell I was new so invited me to a night out after work to get to know people. It turned out the place she told me to meet her was a Brazilian samba bar with 150 Brazilians and I was one of only two English guys in there. I had to pretend I could dance to Samba all night. It was really embarrassing, but at least the 150 Brazilians had a good night laughing at me.

Lunch with Gabi   **Dinner with the Manning Road team**

Gabriela turned out to be one of the best people I met in Sydney. She managed to secure me a room in the house she was living in and I ended up becoming really good friends with her and everyone in the house. 'Manning Road' as it was called, actually became a pretty infamous house in Sydney for parties. We used to host all the parties, all the pre-clubbing parties and all the afterparties which seemed to be on an almost daily basis.

It was like a zoo at times. Hundreds of people walking through the doors every weekend, people who were friends of friends of friends who you'd never met before. I ended up rooming with Victor from France and Fabian from Germany. Now typically, history tells us that there is some tension between a French man, a German man and an English man, however, against all odds these two became my best mates and I still love them to this day.

The unlikely friendship

When it comes to travelling, I always leave things last minute - mainly because I'm very unorganised and a little because I get a buzz from flying off into the unknown with no preparation, not knowing what to expect. But, after hours on Skyscanner and playing around with different airports and using the famed 'flights to everywhere' option I landed on Sydney – Hawaii – Alaska – Canada – Iceland – U.K. or Sydney – Nepal to do EBC (Everest Base Camp), then on to the U.K.

I'd been toying with the idea of doing Base Camp for several years. The last time I was close to booking it was just before the devastating 2015 Earthquake, so I considered

15

myself to be lucky not to have been there that particular year.

I sat down to watch the film *Everest* for some inspiration and booked the flight to leave in two days' time. I didn't think any of it through. Never do. Never learn. I usually get away with it, but you'd have thought I'd have learnt after the India trip where it so nearly went tits up. I'd been sunning it up in Sydney for five months, flip flops weren't going to cut it for the snow and rocky terrain.

India Trip (August 2015): I was at Tomorrowland Festival in Belgium and left myself two days to get a visa sorted in between dancing to Techno music and flying to New Delhi. Long story short (I might write a book about this trip so watch this space – and maybe buy the book, please?), I decided to sign up for the Rickshaw Run – which is racing a beaten up tuk-tuk from north-east India to south-west India in three weeks. Again, I didn't do my research and had to intercept a courier service in Birmingham to fast track my visa. Somehow, I made it but it was the most stressful 'vacation' I have ever had the pleasure of enduring.

Tomorrowland Festival   **Finish line with Sam and Dan**

You can find out more information on how to take part in the Rickshaw Run and other crazy adventures by going to The Adventurists' website (www.theadventurists.com)

TRAVEL TIP: *It's rare I give advice out, but the good/bad advice I would give is - just book what you want to do and work out the rest after, otherwise you may never go.*

Wow, even reading that back sounds ill-advised.

Okay, so I needed hiking gear. My options were buying some in Sydney, which would probably be expensive, buying some in Kathmandu or asking around. Being the bargain hunter that I am, I asked around. Sydney may not be the best place to be asking for winter clothes, but I got lucky. Yes, Richard Frost, the floor guy from work had been to Antarctica.

Family friends of his regularly go on excursions to the South Pole – the southernmost continent. Oh, what it would be like to be one of the privileged. We used to go on regular excursions to Butlin's and it was shit. If you've not heard of Butlin's, it's like Benidorm but with thousands of whinging kids running around. If you've not heard of Benidorm then you're lucky, don't go.

He provided me with the highest quality boots, socks, trousers, jumpers, coat - the lot. I'd only known the guy a few months but he lent me it and just said, "Yeah, give me them back whenever."

Cheers Rich.

**The Frosty siblings -
Legends**

**Clothing provided by
Rich**

After that I exchanged money, bought some balloons to hand out to the local kids on the trail, went to the airport without my laptop, went back to get my laptop, went back to the airport again and I was off. I heard from a friend who had been previously that they gave a balloon to a local kid in the mountains and they got so much enjoyment out of it, so my plan was to give a balloon to every kid that I passed on the way up.

KATHMANDU (1400m)

Winging It

Taking a drone (Phantom Professional 3 model) as hand luggage, presented no preparation problem *numero uno* as I arrived in to Kathmandu Airport. Apparently, you need a license to fly in Nepal and it takes fourteen days to get one. Sound. Book trips in advance kids! What have I been trying to tell you! Anyway, I signed a few papers and left it with security for a couple of weeks. It turned out to be a blessing in disguise as there's no way I was carrying that up to Base Camp with everything else I had to carry.

In 2016 I got a bit excited and bought the drone on finance during the hype. Pretty much a week later they started bringing out drones that were a quarter of the size and fit in your pocket. The camera is 4K and it works great, it's just a nightmare to travel around with.

I was warned about being ripped off by the taxi drivers, but you know when you just don't care? I'd been travelling for what seemed to be a lifetime, I was knackered and just wanted to get there. 2.6 taxi surcharge come at me. I was on my way to Thamel, the tourist hub of Kathmandu, with absolutely nothing booked, no preparation, no sleeping bag and a tight schedule. What could possibly go wrong?

Kathmandu sits in a valley surrounded by the Himalayan mountains. It is a chaotic, yet exciting capital city full of life and is known for being extremely spiritual. Kathmandu is also home to some of the friendliest and most hospitable people on the planet, which I was about to find out. Aside from surviving the carnage on the streets - where there seems to be no set rules or regulations with cars driving in any which way they please - it is a particularly safe place to travel to.

I got some advice from Tom (Famous travel blogger and all-round nice guy who goes by the handle of @traveltomtom), who I had the pleasure of living and hanging out with in Sydney. He had assured me that for the Everest Base Camp trek there was no need to book well in advance and to just book my tour when I get there. I spoke to the taxi driver and he rang his boss who must have had a connection with a tour company. I didn't have a clue what to expect, but for the sake of adventure I thought I may as well give it a try and head to a place they knew.

I was met by a friendly guy named Madan from *Great Vision Trek*. I told him the story of needing to attend a wedding by a certain date and having limited time to get up to EBC and back down, to catch the necessary flight to the U.K. He began constructing a plan for my trip. He was a really helpful guy, and I highly recommend the company. It didn't take long at all to put it together, and he was able to change things around to meet my requirements.

The original price they gave me was US $1250, which to be honest, is very reasonable. I met a lot of people who paid more than that, but I knew I could reduce the price even further. I removed the cost of food and drinks from the itinerary and instead of hiring a guide from Kathmandu and flying him over with me I picked up a guide in Lukla on arrival. I managed to get the price down to $800. They also kept my suitcase in their office free of charge for almost two weeks.

I never did the maths, but I'm pretty sure I saved money by buying my own food and drink.

TRAVEL TIP: You don't need to book in advance. You don't need a guide. There are a lot of people walking the same way who you could follow.
BUT I highly recommend getting one! Especially if something goes wrong. Weather conditions can be rough up there, e.g. when it's foggy you can barely see your hand in front of your face at times, so if something happens to you no one can even see you.

By chance, Phil – a British guy who I met on the Rickshaw Run - was staying in a nearby hostel and trekking in the area, so Madan called me a tuk-tuk to get me to the hostel. There was a bit of miscommunication here. After three weeks racing across India, I said I could drive tuk-tuks so Madan told the tuk-tuk driver I would drive.

Tuk-tuks in Nepal do not have the same meaning as tuk-tuks in India. I don't even know how to describe the thing that turned up. It looked like a penny-farthing on acid, and made worse by the fact you had to balance it with a wooden stick to stop it from toppling over. Told you I didn't know how to describe it.

A Nepalese tuk-tuk   **Everest Lager**

After checking into the hostel (*Alobar1000 Hostel*), I made my way to the bar where Phil greeted me with a large Everest lager. 'Everest' is one of the local beers in the area and I can confirm it tastes unbelievable after a long, hard day of travelling and stress.

Phil told me that he had been volunteering for the disaster relief charity *All Hands* (www.hands.org), a volunteer-powered disaster relief organisation dedicated to rebuilding hope for people impacted by natural disasters.

I first met Phil when we played football with the Rickshaw Run participants versus the local press in Shillong, on the first day of the trip. We drew 3-3 thanks to goals from myself and Phil who scored a 30-yard screamer.

We got on well and stayed in touch thanks to Mark Zuckerberg.

Back in Nepal, I joined Phil and his mates for a meal, followed by a wander through the streets of Thamel. I thought it was a really cool vibe at night, there seemed to be excitement in the air, all the shops were lit up and people could be seen shopping for their last few bits before trekking. You could spot the professionals a mile off. They had a certain look about them and a swagger when they walked, which was a fair description if you're attempting to summit the highest mountain in the world. Before we debated having another beer, we headed back for an early night, ready for the 5 am start.

You can read Phil's blogs by heading to this page – (www.seriesofadjustments.wordpress.com)

TRAVEL TIP: Always exchange details with the people you meet! It's one of the many great things about travelling. You meet someone, even if it's just for five minutes and you won't know when or where, but there's a chance you may cross paths again.

I had the same discussion with my former housemate 'traveltomtom' before I left to Nepal. The more you travel and meet people, the more connections and places you have to stay around the world – essentially saving you loads of money.

In this instance, I was travelling alone so it was good to meet up with Phil and his mates and have someone to show me around Kathmandu and go for dinner with. Another recent example is an Italian guy I met called Massimo. I met him very briefly whilst climbing Sigiriya Rock in Sri Lanka. We exchanged details as he said he was heading to Australia at some point. A few months later he got in touch and said he was heading to Sydney from Melbourne and looking for work. I managed to set him up with a job and a place to live; ready for the day he arrived.

Now he's in my debt so he owes me one. See you in Italy soon Massimo.

Me, Tom and Massimo

What was included in the package for the $800:

Guide: Albeit too fast, the guide leads you safely up to Everest Base Camp and back down. They check you into the lodges, organise your food and make sure your timings are managed. Especially in Ngima's case, he helped me make important decisions about my safety, which is crucial.

Permits: The guide keeps all the documents and deals with all the border crossings.

Accommodation: The price included lodges for the duration of the trip. Where you stay is usually down to the guide and who he is friends or family with. This is a good thing, as it means you are well looked after.

Return flights: From Kathmandu to Lukla.

Transfer: From the tour company to the hotel.

Transfer: From the hotel to the airport

Luggage storage: Storage of anything you don't need for the trek is kept at the office. In my case it was a giant suitcase. Bargain if you ask me.

Taxi information:

- During the day time, the taxi from the airport to Thamel (where the majority of the hostels and travel companies are located) is around 45 minutes to 1 Hour. This is due to how bad the traffic is at this time.

- During the night through to early morning the taxi from Thamel to the airport is only around 15 minutes. The streets were empty when I travelled to the airport.

- The price of the taxi one way was around $7 for me (You can get it for $4, but I was too tired to care), or free if it is part of your trekking or hotel package.

KATHMANDU (1400m) to LUKLA (2860m) to PHAKDING (2610m)

Landing in the Most Dangerous Airport in the World

Boarding, Kathmandu

I started the day by taking a nice, bonny, little, petite plane from Kathmandu to Lukla. It was anything but, as it consisted of half an hour of turbulence and screaming. It was impossible to enjoy the view because one minute you'll be looking at the mountains, then next you're forced to look at the looming ground as the plane flapped in the wind. Approaching the most dangerous airport in the world was exactly as traumatic as it sounds. If the pilot misses the abrupt turn at the end of the incredibly short runway, the plane will crash into the wall. One of the locals told me that this airport in the mountains loses - on average - four planes a year.

In-Flight Safety Briefing   **View of the Himalayas**

I was sitting at the back of the plane so couldn't see the runway approaching. We were struck by a large bang which came out of nowhere as we touched the 527m-long (or short) runway. This was followed by a hard break, before making the necessary turn into a parking space. I can't possibly call it a terminal, it looked more like a supermarket carpark.

Ngima (pronounced "Nee-ma"), my guide, must have Facebook stalked me as he spotted me straight away coming off the plane. He grabbed me and said, "Follow me" and led me to his family's house. We had some food, courtesy of his mother in law and I charged my phone. I think it only went from 64% to 67% in the time we were there.

World's most dangerous airport

Lukla, sitting at 2860 metres

TRAVEL TIP: Bring a couple of power banks. It's definitely worth using them, rather than relying on the electricity there. It's not the strongest, and in most places it's quite expensive to use. I'd recommend the Anker Power Bank (www.anker.com). I think I got mine for around $40 on Amazon. I bought it for Glastonbury Festival and I think it charged my phone five times and it still had more charge left in it.

Lukla is a small, crowded town with extraordinary views of the neighbouring mountains. Local businesses are packed side by side, all the way up the high street. The shops were overflowing with Everest merchandise and hiking gear, as they tried to make their last sales before the tourists set off on the trail. You could sense the energy in the town, with big beaming smiles wherever you looked. I'm not sure if this was in anticipation of the trek or a sign of relief at surviving the world's most dangerous airport.

After checking out the local shops and stocking up on some drinks and energy snacks, we began the 8km trek down to Phakding. Other than coming down from Base Camp, this would be the only time where we would be finishing a day at a lower altitude to where we started. Apart from adjusting to the breathing at high altitude, this was a relatively easy walk, made easier by the spectacular views as we made our way down into the valley. Remember I flew from near sea level in Sydney, to Kathmandu, which is 1400 metres, then on to Lukla, which is 2860 metres - all this in a space of 24 hours.

Downhill walk through the valley

Picturesque bridge

Ngima is either the most famous man in Nepal or he does this trek a lot. Probably both. He seemed to know every single local person we passed, acknowledging them all with a greeting, walking and talking with them. When we eventually arrived in Phakding he had beers and played pool with them all. I felt a bit left out. I think he forgot about me...

When I did actually get a chance to have a chat with him, he began to tell me about the earthquake of 2015 and his story - where he was, and how it affected him and his family. Fortunately, none of his family were killed in the disaster, but life was really difficult for them. He told me that he, his wife and daughter lived in a tent for a full year after the earthquake.

The earthquake is believed to have affected the lives of more than 8 million people - nearly one third of Nepal's population. 200,000 people are thought to have been displaced from their homes, with many still living in temporary shelters due to how slow the recovery has been.

Ngima - man with the map

The line of work he is in actually helped, as he received aid from people, he had previously guided. They contacted him through social media. He also told me how he had been trying to get a visa for Australia for some time, but has not had any success. At the end of the year I was moving back to Dubai, so I said I would make some enquiries there for him.

I don't know if this is scientifically accurate or scientifically stupid, but I lost my inhaler in the run up to this trip. I needed to find a solution. The answer came to me whilst sat on the plane. I looked out the window to the stars, looked up to God... even looked at a perplexed flight attendant, who was too busy bashing people's knees with the aisle trolley. Then, out of nowhere, it came to me - a pure blessing, when I thought all hope was lost, I saw a creased sick bag folded over the back of the inconsiderate 'I'll recline back as far as possible' dickhead's chair.

In laymen's terms – I took the sick bag to use as a replacement inhaler.

I headed to one of the local bars to use the free Wi-Fi. I wasn't planning on using the Wi-Fi, especially on the first day but I couldn't find a book and travelling alone was proving lonely. I get on with myself, I'm decent craic, but after a while you need another human to converse with, or something to occupy your time, such as reading. As good as the views are you do get bored!

Phakding football pitch   **Dudh Kosi river**

It turned out this Wi-Fi was free because it didn't work, so it was back to my room to stare at the wall and write this book. I tried to guess a few Wi-Fi passwords in the area – e.g. 123Phakding, Everest1, Cantbreathe2017 etc. but no luck.

Unfortunately - or fortunately depending on your preference - you do in fact have to squat in most toilets. Earlier in the day, I said to myself, the cattle are disgusting flicking their shit everywhere. I was doing the same two hours later when I got to the lodge. Hand on the wall for balance, flicking my white ass.

TRAVEL TIP: *Buy constipation pills.*
That was a joke. Don't do that.

It only took the first night to discover just how cold it gets. In the daytime when the sun is out, it's hot, with a nice cool wind if you're lucky. It's a totally different story at night. When I was writing my last-minute checklist, I managed to write down balloons but not a sleeping bag. I managed to borrow another sheet/duvet/cloth/tea towel, I don't know what you would call it and wore all of my clothes to survive the night. I'm talking woolly hat, gloves, three t-shirts, three jumpers, coat, underwear, two pairs of shorts, two pairs of leggings, waterproof trousers, three pairs of socks. Oh, and a pair of hiking boots. I chose these over the Nike trainers as they covered my ankles and let less of a draft in.

The next stop was Namche Bazaar – this is the last place where you can buy hiking gear, so my plan was to buy a sleeping bag there.

During the spring, the temperature in Phakding ranges from around 5 degrees Celsius to 20 degrees Celsius in the day time and around -5 degrees Celsius to 5 degrees Celsius at night.

TREKKING TIP: Keep regulating your body temperature. I was always pulling my sleeves or trousers up and down, taking my hat off or on etc. The sun and a change in winds make a massive difference. With the wind it can feel very cold, but you can actually be getting severely sunburnt without realising – wear sun cream! I was aiming to have five or six litres of water a day - as recommended by a guide. A lot of people I met weren't taking in anywhere near that and they were getting ill so I'd aim for five or six.

Phakding Prices (In Nepalese rupee):

Full mobile phone charge = 200
Wi-Fi = 300 per hour or 500 per day
Water = 100
Bottle of Coca Cola= 300
Meal = Ranges from 400 to 600
Tea = 60

Staring at the wall to pass the time thoughts:

- Would I get more out of travelling alone?

Up until now, it had been nice being in my own head and having that space and separation from society and noise. When you're hiking in the Himalayas in crisp, fresh air, with magnificent views I can assure you that there is no stress or pressures that you are so accustomed to, when living in a city.

Also, I am usually all for travelling with new people and there would be many positives of travelling in a big group. However, with the large groups you are all different paces and at different fitness levels. There is the likelihood that people will get ill at certain points and the Sherpas or guides that you may rely on, could have to return to lower altitude with those who cannot go on. There is also the possibility that you could be paired with someone really bloody annoying who doesn't stop talking. You know who you are.

- *Six or seven hours to Namche Bazaar is going to be tough!*

- *It's an incredibly steep climb up to Namche Bazaar. It's difficult as it is, never mind that with every step into higher altitude you're breathing in less and less oxygen.*

- *Don't worry about the cost of things. The money is helping those that suffered from the earthquake.*

I started to think I was being ripped off, and then I quickly corrected myself. It's not just the fact that the money is going to families who need it, but if anywhere should be expensive it's five thousand metres up a mountain. Sherpas trek for days, carrying all this food and equipment on their backs from Lukla, so go ahead - increase those prices. Meanwhile, Marks & Spencer's back home are charging £4.25 for a salad, which has been delivered in a nice, air-conditioned Mercedes van.

- *Will people bother reading my book?*

- *Well, you've come this far.*

- *Am I worried about dying?*

Yep, but I would never tell anyone else that.

PHAKDING (2610m) to NAMCHE BAZAAR (3440m)

The Swinging Bridge of Death

I woke up at 5:30 am and it was absolutely baltic!

It's a real-life experience when you go on a 'holiday' where you're trying to balance enjoying yourself with staying   alive.

I headed downstairs for my jam on toast. You forget you're surrounded by these colossal mountains wherever you look. Unfortunately, I haven't been yet, but the views reminded me of, or how I imagine Canada to be like. Ngima gave me a quick brief of today's route and we were off. Destination: Namche Bazaar.

It was a fairly steady incline for the first few hours. This was until we arrived at two questionable bridges (visible in the 2015 *Everest* movie) - high up, dangling over these glacial river rapids. I didn't even take much notice of the higher one as I just assumed that we wouldn't be crossing that one.

But we were. We'd crossed a few similar bridges on the first day and a half but they were nowhere near that high. We made our way up there and as I arrived there was one guy on his knees having a bit of an episode. The poor guy had not made it across. It looked like he'd had a panic attack or something - which is completely understandable considering the sheer height of the drop. Luckily, he had a friend by his side calming him down and after a few minutes he looked to be just about okay.

| Suspension bridges | First few cautious steps across |

TRAVEL TIP: As advised by a Dutch guy I met at this bridge - wear shades! At high altitude especially, the sun can make you severely ill if you keep catching it in your vision all day. Mine broke so I promised to buy some new ones in Namche.

Knowing the guy was okay, I took my first few steps across. Despite the bridge literally swinging in the wind I felt fine. I've always been a bit of an adrenalin junkie. I get a buzz out of fear; and conquering it. My first ever memory is my dad putting me on his shoulders in a South American water park and going down a slide into a pool.

He also made a giant swing that you could push from inside the house and it would swing me out of the doorway above the traffic on the road - so I guess I'm used to it. People would literally look out of their car windows and see a flying baby come towards them over the top of a hedge, every three to four seconds. This was back in the '90s when safety didn't exist.

Homemade swing	**Hoping it doesn't snap**

You think you are fine, then you look down and see bolts missing from the metal strips and see how fucking high up you are, with the ice-cold rapids below. It was like something from Indiana Jones. I could have just run across with my hands over my eyes, but I had to get some footage. I turned around to go back and come across again and one of the locals, carrying half of Phakding, came running at me, across the bridge. He was carrying a large wooden door of some sort across his shoulders. A *Nepalese Buzz-Lightyear* was running at me across a bridge. He would've literally taken my head off. I dived to my right, to the floor and managed to find the only gap.

With my head still attached, I began the vertical climb up to Namche. I was finding the altitude manageable up to this point. You can really start to feel the effect of the altitude once you start climbing rather than walking. I'd say every four or five minutes I was stopping and giving myself a breather. The guide was going so fast, I couldn't keep up. It's easy to become frustrated with yourself that you can't go any quicker, but after a while I decided it was better just to go at my own pace. If you try and match someone else, especially a local guide who lives at this altitude you can face serious issues very quickly.

The sound of helicopter blades became more and more frequent, regularly flying overhead to remind you of the danger. Altitude sickness is serious business in Nepal. Whilst some are carrying cargo, many are rescue helicopters getting people suffering from Acute Mountain Sickness (AMS) down the mountain - and at a cost. If you don't have insurance a fifteen-minute ride to safety can set you back up to five thousand dollars.

Again, down to lack of organisation, I realised my insurance only covered me up to 3000 metres. I ended up spending an additional $200 on insurance to cover me up to 6000 metres. This also included helicopter rescue. I met people who had cheaper insurance, but I didn't leave myself a lot time to do much price comparison and research.

At around the halfway stage from the 'Bridge of Death' up to Namche, we passed the first Everest viewpoint. By chance I bumped into the guy I had sat next to on the plane, an American guy volunteering to build a school where they train guides and Sherpas. After lunch the weather usually turns. It tends to be really clear in the morning, then clouds over in the afternoon. Unfortunately, it was the afternoon and the thick, grey clouds were spoiling the view. I would have to wait a bit longer to tick off one of my dreams - seeing the world's highest peak.

My guide was literally 'The Bullshit Man'. I don't know if it was an ingenious way to get me up the mountains and keep me going but he'd always say "yes, just another twenty minutes" when really there was two to three hours left. The other guide I kept bumping into was 'The Fact Man'. If I had any queries that needed factual responses, I would ask him.

After a three or four-hour (or twenty minute) battle in the heat, I made it to the next village. The last real market town for mountaineering gear, and in my case, a sleeping bag! I wandered around and similar to Lukla, noticed that there were snooker tables everywhere. It must be the national sport. Ngima said he spends a lot of his evenings playing with his mates and fellow guides. Unfortunately, my hands were too cold to play.

Also, to my delight, they had proper toilets. Success!

The colourful Namche Bazaar

At 3500 metres Namche Bazaar is a popular acclimatisation spot for trekkers. Tour companies and guides recommend stopping here for two nights, as there are plenty of bars, cafes and restaurants to enjoy, as well as easy-going hikes in the surrounding areas. Having acclimatisation days is vital, as I found out later in the trip.

I settled in at the lodge and got talking to *Spanish surfer girl* Merie, who had been living in Australia. I was surprised at how good my Spanish was. It's not good, but I could at least converse. Merie was probably just nodding and smiling out of sympathy actually.

"Hola, mi Llamo Cory, mi familia vivo en Chile, con mi padre y mi madre y no perro."

(Hello, my name is Cory, my family live in Chile, with my father and my mother and not a dog)

That was my oral exam from year 10 at school. I just repeat that every time I meet a Spanish person.

Probably why I got a D.

It was becoming dark and cold, which meant it was time to buy a sleeping bag. Unfortunately, none of the ATM's accepted MasterCard. I lost my Visa card in Sydney, involving a bottle of Fireball, a 40-year old Columbian and Transvestite Bingo.

Shit.

I managed to exchange my remaining dollars ($100 got me 9800 Nepalese rupees) so I had enough to get me by for the next day or two. But there was no way I had enough money left to stay alive for the rest of the trip, let alone, enough to buy a sleeping bag. The nights were sleepless as they were. Now I'm lying awake with frostbite, worrying about money.

TRAVEL TIP: *Always have plenty of dollars on you. You can always exchange dollars wherever you are.*

Wi-Fi at this joint was 100 Nepalese rupees an hour, which isn't bad. Yes, it is nice to have time away from social media influencers, clickbait headlines and seeing a scarcity of Tinder matches, but having Wi-Fi does pass the time when you're sitting around (Or buy a book. Buy a book). It was a good time to contact family, sort insurance out and contact 'Rickshaw Run Phil', so we could meet up the following day.

Namche Bazaar Prices (In Nepalese rupee):

To charge mobile phone = 100 per hour
Bottle of Coke = 350
Bottle of Water = 150
Meal = 550
Soup = 300
Jam on Toast = 250
Chocolate Bar = 100

NAMCHE BAZAAR (3440m) to EVEREST VIEW POINT (3840m)
Vertigo Infused Anxiety Attack

Wake up time - 5:30 am
Breakfast - 6:30 am
Time to leave – 7:00 am

Views for days. Literally. +6000 metre, snow-capped mountains on my door step to wake up to. I shared a coffee with Takashi, a 57-year-old Japanese guy who was travelling alone. I befriended him as he had been staying in the same lodges as me so far on the trip. We discussed the POA for the day. The plan was to head up another four hundred metres to a viewpoint and hopefully catch our first sight of Everest.

I remembered as a child I would be excited every day wondering what adventures I would experience, but in terms of adulthood excitement, I think the last time I was this exhilarated was the first time I went to Tomorrowland. It may be quite shameful comparing a festival to hiking the world's biggest mountain, but I was bloody giddy. This would surely top it though.

Tomorrowland main stage, 2012

I had never taken so many photos in such a short space of time (in fact, it turned out to be the most photos I took on one day), as we hiked up to the Everest View Point. You were surrounded by all these mountains up to eight thousand metres tall. It was so overwhelming. We passed what was once the world's highest airport - Syangboche Airport. The run-down airstrip that sits just above Namche Bazaar, is the closest airstrip to Mount Everest, but as it no longer has a commercial license it is now only used by helicopters making stops in-between Lukla and Everest Base Camp.

Moments later, a helicopter landed at our feet and with the sun coming up from behind a seven thousand metre peak, a picturesque teahouse on the hill shimmered in the distance.

Syangboche Airport

Surrounded by colossal mountains

Helicopter lands at 3800 metres

Teahouse on the hill

I can't even explain the next bit.

Well I'll try. After blood, sweat, tears and no beers (yet) I had made it to the first clear viewpoint. I can see Everest. I'm there. I feel like I have summited.

I never imagined it to be as dramatic as it actually was. I literally had some kind of vertigo infused anxiety attack where I was unable to look at it. I went all wobbly and had to turn around and sit down. I had finally made it, a genuine life-long dream of mine and I had to sit with my back to the view, having a complete loss of equilibrium and feeling unbelievably light headed.

My head just went – "Noooooo. Mountains. Bad."

After shedding off a few light twitches and composing myself, I was able to turn around and just absorb the scenery. And from then on, I couldn't stop. It was just fucking amazing. I had tingling chills running through my body, in a complete state of euphoria.

First view of Everest (peak on the left)   **Me and my mate Everest**

We climbed a bit further and made it to the 'Hotel Everest View' (www.hoteleverestview.com), former Guinness World Record's highest hotel in the world. The hotel, which opened in 1971 is a popular destination for the acclimatisation hike from Namche Bazaar and reveals incredible panoramic views of the Himalayas.

I bumped into Takashi and we had a few photos together and exchanged contacts - which ended up becoming really handy for when I stopped in Japan on the way to Australia! I felt bad not ordering anything, so I decided to test the Garlic Soup, which had been recommended to me by the locals to help with altitude sickness.

Takashi and me   **Panoramic view from Hotel Everest View**

EVEREST TREKKING TIP: Make sure you read the small print at this hotel as they add 25% tax on to the bill here.

Thankfully I ordered the cheapest thing on the menu.

Garlic Soup has natural properties that help you when suffering from Acute Mountain Sickness (AMS). Your blood gets thicker at high altitude and Garlic thins out your blood. It is recommended to have at least one bowl of Garlic Soup per day when trekking in the mountains.

I was still hungry so we pretty much ran back down to Namche and I ordered the usual - Dahl. Bargain of the week - unlimited Dahl, Rice and other bits for 550 rupees. Following lunch, I had another stroll around the markets to try find some new gloves (I think I left mine in Phakding), some cheap souvenirs and then I walked up a hill for some half price Fanta. It really wasn't worth saving the equivalent of 50 pence, as I was absolutely knackered by the time I got there. I was so dehydrated and out of breath that I necked it in one. Took me forever getting up there and it was gone within three seconds. After picking up a couple of EBC and Nepal t-shirts I came across The Holy Grail.

Of course, there's an Irish Bar! Apparently, the highest Irish Bar in the world. You can tell it's not your usual Irish Bar, as outside I could see a Yak being slapped by a kid, shortly followed by a kid being chased and slapped by an elderly woman. Yaks are sacred animals here, so it is forbidden to hit them.

Highest Irish Bar in the world

I arranged to meet Phil and his mate Jesse at the bar over a beer and a few games of pool. I did my best. I lasted the best part of three days. If the shakes weren't from the brisk cold winds, then it was probably due to the lack of alcohol intake.

Apart from watching Man City win on the big projector screen, it was a good night and good to spend some time with other humans. Phil and his group were taking a different route to me so we said our goodbyes and agreed to meet up again somewhere in the future.

It was getting late so I went back to the lodge. This turned out to be the best lodge for food that I stayed in. The accommodation you stay in is usually the tour guides friends/family, which is cool, and means you are well looked after. They managed to cook me up a delicious cheese and

45

tomato pizza, giving my taste buds a break from the dahl and spices. It was so good I ended up having it again for my 6 am breakfast the next day.

EVEREST TREKKING TIP: It is very important that you eat breakfast, lunch and dinner at your lodge. It is to be expected and both you and your guide can get fined if they catch you eating elsewhere.

TRAVEL TIP: Buy water purification tablets in Kathmandu. I was recommended not to use them till I reached my target of EBC just in case I became sick, but many of the people that I met were using them from the start to the end of the climb.

I went for my first shower since I left Kathmandu. It was fucking freezing! It wasn't so much the water; it was the ice-cold floor. I couldn't even stand on it. I had to jump out and back into the corridor onto the wooden flooring. I needed an alternative. I wet my football shorts, stood in the bedroom and scrubbed all the dirt and sweat off my skin. Life.

Choose life. Choose trekking. Choose a mountain. Choose a fucking freezing climate. Choose not to bring a sleeping bag. Choose a sick bag rather than an inhaler. Choose the wrong insurance. Choose life.

Staring at the wall to pass the time thoughts:

I'm really worried about money now. I don't have enough to make it to the end of the trip.

I was genuinely not sure what I was going to do. I was travelling alone, so there was no one I could borrow money off and as much as I'd have loved to, I didn't have time to take paid work sherpa'ing.

- *No more snacks or fizzy drinks - they're too expensive.*

I rationalised that I would have to budget by not purchasing any more fizzy drinks or snacks. I never thought it would get to the point where I couldn't afford a can of Fanta – even the half-priced stuff up the hill. Just dahl and tea for the rest of the trip it seemed.

NAMCHE BAZAAR (3440m) to TENGBOCHE (3860m)

Squaring up to a Mountain Goat

Day four and I'm still in my Nike trainers.

TRAVEL TIP: Comfortable trainers are fine (unless you're really unlucky with the weather). I would actually recommend these. I didn't get any blisters; you don't have to wear them in and they are fairly lightweight.

I kept bumping into this girl from Sydney. I saw her again fairly soon after I left the lodge, so shouted "Hey Sydney." I'm not sure if that's offensive or not, but I forgot her name. Jasmine took it well and we got to know each other a bit better and walked some of the way together before lunch. There weren't many other people trekking alone, so I had a lot of respect for her, as I know it's tough.

As we stopped for lunch, I noticed how it was starting to get more and more expensive the further up you get. I accepted that the prices had to be marked up, I was just hoping that I wouldn't have to pay fifty dollars for a dahl by the time I got to Base Camp. Despite the increased prices, lunch was in a really beautiful spot down in the valley. The river ran through the middle of the village, so the sound of the flowing water and wildlife was really peaceful.

After lunch, however, I had the shock of my life. This massive rogue mountain goat was right on the other side of this tree as I came around the corner. We both shat ourselves. I startled him and he startled me. We both legged it in opposite directions. When your heart beats fast at high altitude it feels like a time bomb. Looking back, it's hilarious but at the time it was traumatic. I didn't have enough time to register what it was. They're very unpredictable and peculiar creatures. They're like the weird guy at the after party. They're harmless but you know you should stay away from them.

Ngima told me it was not as busy as the previous few months, so in that respect. May is a good time to go. You especially notice it when you are crossing bridges as you can nearly always just walk straight across. During the busy periods however, you have to wait for group after group of people to get across before you can move onto the bridge.

Donkey traffic

I thought the climb to Namche was ruthless... this was literally climbing up vertically. It was so tough. My knees and shoulders were giving me a lot of grief. We were exposed to the sun for the whole climb as well, there was no shade for miles. I noticed Ngima helping one of his friends that was struggling. He was holding hands with him, making sure he was okay. He was helping his mates more than me! I'm not saying I wanted him to hold my hand, but I was dying man!

We finally found a litterbin that provided a few people with a bit of shade. I met a cool couple from Canada at the *garbage chill out area*. I'm sick of saying, "Where are you guys from?" when you meet people, but it's the only chat I've got and I guess it's a good ice breaker. More often than not the people you meet will have some useful information or tips to help you on the journey.

As I looked around, I noticed more helicopters overhead - another reminder that I'm a dickhead doing it on my own, with no sleeping bag and no money.

I also noticed a group of sherpa women carrying the size of my dad's hoarding collection up this cliff face. My mum struggles with her Tesco bag, bless her - and the supermarket is only around the corner! The sherpas here are like superhumans, it is mind-boggling how they can carry so much stuff on their backs.

Surrounded by magnificent views of Everest, Tawache, Nuptse, Lhotse, Ama Dablam and Thamserku, I had made it to Tengboche. Located at 3,800m, the village is home to the Tengboche Monastery - one of the most significant Buddhist monasteries in the Khumbu Region. Tenzing Norgay, the first man to climb to the summit of Mount Everest with Sir Edmund Hilary in 1953, was known to have lived in Tengboche.

It was starting to get late and a storm was brewing at Tengboche. High winds swept through the village,

49

generating a sort of sandstorm picked up from all the dirt, to the point where you could not go outside. Despite this, there was still no sign of my 57-year-old mate from Tokyo.

I didn't even know the bloke, but I was starting to get a bit worried about him. I kept walking up to the top of the village to look down the paths to see if he was anywhere close by. Finally, at 7:30pm he arrived. Seven hours after me! I felt bad about him; I didn't think I was going particularly fast, so he must have been really struggling.

Stroke of luck! My cash problem was solved. It was too late to buy a sleeping bag, but I managed to get cash back at the hotel (The Mountain Paradise Lodge), when I paid my bill. It was meant to be with a 10% fee but the owners' son did it for 8%. It was run by a really nice family and I had an in-depth chat on the roof with the owner, an elderly guy who had lived there his whole life. He had so many stories from his time running the hotel. Too many for now unfortunately. I'm already up to ten thousand words.

And so are you if you're reading this.

Tengboche Prices (In Nepalese Rupee):

To charge mobile phone = 300 per hour
Bottle of Coca Cola = 400
Bottle of Water = 200
Dahl (with unlimited top-up) = 700
Wi-Fi (200mb) = 600
Jam on Toast = 300

TENGBOCHE (3860m) to DINGBOCHE (4410m)
2-4-1 Sunrise

Double sunrise, Tengboche

Waking up in Tengboche meant waking up to the best sunrise I have ever seen, I even got two for the price of one. Due to the sheer size of Everest, the reflection created a second sun.

The balloons I bought in Sydney finally got to make an appearance as we stopped for lunch at one of Ngima's friend's place. The couple were parents to this hilarious, crazy kid who couldn't speak much English, but whom I got on really well with.

He'd be standing on the wall of his restaurant shouting, teasing and throwing things at passers-by who were struggling up the hill. I thought this would be the perfect opportunity to give him some balloons to play with.

His dad blew one up for him, and out of nowhere he broke out into the English version of "Happy Birthday" waving his balloon around. I couldn't believe it.

The kid later requested that we sit at the table together and we both enjoyed his mum's spaghetti before I was on my way. He made my day and I hope I made his.

51

The performer **Mum's spaghetti at 4000 metres**

The sun continued to make the trek more difficult than it needed to be, as the heat really takes it out of you. There's no hiding from it really. You just need to make sure you're constantly hydrated.

Due to all the photos and videos on my iPhone I didn't have much room for music. I think I chose about twenty tracks and I hadn't got sick of any of them so far. Choose wisely, it helps unless you pick a selection of annoying chart music 'hits' that you'll get sick of. I'm talking about work by lyrical geniuses such as Nicky Minaj, with her chart topper (please stop her) – "Anaconda." If I was more organised, I would have bought an iPod and a Kindle or something.

Just as Ngima was telling me about a young French guy that died the previous year, falling off the metre-wide cliff we were on, a herd of Yak's (if you can call it a herd) crossed our path. I was literally hanging on to the cliff face, clinging onto some loose rocks while hoping the Yak's didn't have some sort of claustrophobic fit and shunt me off the path.

We finally arrived in Dingboche, situated at 4400m, which meant it was the highest anyone in my family had ever climbed. I even surpassed my dad, Ian, who summited a major peak in the Andes, South America. I did ask him which one but he said "I can't remember, one near Aconcagua." Aconcagua (6960m) boasts the highest peak in the Americas and is the second highest of the Seven Summits (highest mountains in each continent).

Arriving in Dingboche also meant it was higher than La Paz, Bolivia (3600m) and Machu Picchu, Peru (2400m) - two places with high altitude that I visited in 2011 during my three months backpacking.

When I arrived at the lodge, I noticed everyone drying their clothes on the rooftops. I knew my clothes smelt bad, but the higher you get up into the mountains the more likely the weather is to turn, meaning you don't have very long to dry anything. I went for a second whiff. They smelt really fucking bad. They desperately needed washing, so I gave them a wash in the sink and put them out to dry. It was glorious sunshine. No dramas.

The weather really does turn 'ey?

The unwelcome arrival of a hail storm pounded on the rooftops. The clothes were wet from the sweat, but now they're soaking wet.

A snowy Dingboche

53

Once the weather piped down, I went for a stroll. I tend to just go on walks on my own to pass the time. It was quite peaceful but I really would've liked someone else to chill with. Once you strip away people and the Internet from your life, it's like "Shit, what the fuck do I do!?"

As darkness fell, I was hoping to see Jasmine again, as she seemed cool and there was still no sign of Takashi. I headed back to the lodge. After entertaining myself for almost a week, a group of Kiwis welcomed me over to their table to join in with their card game. You really start to appreciate just having a conversation and a laugh with other people after travelling alone for so long.

Dingboche Prices (In Nepalese rupee):

Bottle of Water = 250
Bottle of Coke = 350
Most meals on the menu = 400
Black Tea = 100
Dahl (with unlimited top-up) = 550
Wi-Fi = 600

After several games of cards, I made my way back to my room and pondered over the next few days.

Staring at the wall to pass the time thoughts:

- *Can I skip a day in Dingboche?*

The careless thinking behind me skipping an acclimatisation day was "I'm macho, I feel fine so far... nothing can stop me." If I skipped an acclimatisation day, I could get to the base camp sooner and then get back down earlier.

- *Can I get from EBC to Lukla in two days?*

I was told that in order to have any chance of changing my flight to an earlier one, it would mean I would literally have to run down from Everest Base Camp to Lukla Airport. With the weather getting progressively worse, it was getting more and more likely that flights would be delayed out of Lukla and I needed to make this wedding! If I arrived back in four days - which is the usual descent time, then it would be impossible to catch my international flight from Kathmandu.

If Everest didn't kill me, I knew my mum would if I missed this wedding.

Me being me, I decided to go ahead with the climb the next day and ignore the original advice I'd been given about how important acclimatisation days were.

In the spring, the temperature in Dingboche ranges anywhere from -5 degrees Celsius to 15 degrees Celsius in the day time and around -15 degrees Celsius to -5 degrees Celsius at night.

DINGBOCHE (4410m) TO LOBUCHE (4940m) – FIRST ATTEMPT

Lack of Brain Cells

I'm blaming the lack of oxygen for my lack of brain cells whilst staying in Dingboche. Not only did I decide to skip a day of acclimatisation, but I had left my boxers out to dry overnight and when I went to check on them in the morning, they were just ice blocks, completely frozen.

This would be the last time I attempted to wash my clothes in the Himalayas.

As it was getting colder and colder as each day went by, I decided that I would start doing warm ups and stretches every morning to get the blood flowing before hiking. This was in the hope that it would warm me up and also prepare my muscles for all the exercise.

Throughout the journey I had picked up some useful advice from other trekkers, however, on this particular part of the climb on day six, I realised that the advice – "Go at your own pace" is terrible, dangerous advice. By going at my own pace in fact nearly hospitalised me. I headed out at what I thought to be a steady pace, not too fast, the pace I had been going the whole trip. However, now that I was at more than 4000m, this meant that there was now 40% less oxygen than at sea level. Considering I spend half my time below sea level in basement raves this was problematic.

I remember clearly saying to myself "I don't even feel that bad, I don't know what I was worried about" and literally within thirty seconds I started to feel dizzy and that *opposite of vertigo*, infused anxiety attack came back and I felt weak and breathless. At this point there was a storm brewing. With the approaching heavy fog, I couldn't see further than a few steps in front of me and my guide was nowhere to be seen. I knew he was a good guy and I was confident he would stop to let me catch up once he realised I wasn't behind.

Now with a piercing headache, every step was frustratingly challenging. This was something I had never felt before. This was altitude sickness! It felt like a lifetime till I got to Ngima. We sat down for around twenty minutes and discussed what the plan of action should be. I felt slightly embarrassed that I couldn't go on, even though I felt like I should risk it, but this is where having a guide is very important.

He looked at me and said I looked pale, like ill pale not English pale. Then he told me that if I was to continue the climb, it would result in me being taken to the nearest hospital in a rescue helicopter. That really made the decision for me. I had to descend to a lower altitude - and fast.

It was difficult walking back past the people I'd previously met and having to explain to them why I was heading back down the mountain. I felt demoralised knowing I would have to take those same steps again the following day if I wanted to make it to EBC. As we set off back, the thick fog turned to snow and a blizzard began to sweep through the valley. I was in a deflated mood as it was, so getting twatted in the face repeatedly by ice wasn't helping. The only bonus to come out of this was that I didn't have to walk in it all day.

The blizzard ended up lasting for six hours.

For the first time on the trip I was very concerned for my own health. I took my first altitude sickness pill – Diamox.

Once I returned to the lodge, I spent three hours hugging the fire - head-to-toe in warm clothing gear and yet I was still shivering, not getting any warmer. The headache hadn't gone away and I was feeling nauseous. I ordered a garlic soup and a Mars bar for energy and made sure I had a regular intake of water.

Morale was low until an Indian couple by the names of Priyanka and Kunal, along with their dancing sherpa arrived back from EBC to the lodge. They got me involved in a new card game and were absolutely hilarious. I think the laughing must have warmed me up and I forgot about how bad I felt.

Priyanka and Kunal in the Dingboche Lodge

They'd just made it back after camping overnight at EBC with some of the summiteers and they described to me about some of the luxuries the guys at Base Camp have. Obviously, it's still tough being up there for months, but they had access to televisions, heaters, charge plugs, imported food, doctors on call with state-of-the-art medical facilities and other things to keep the mountaineers connected with life back home. They also mentioned how a woman, who was there with her father, collapsed at Base Camp.

The number of deaths on the Everest Base Camp trek are typically quite low – somewhere around three to six per year. Most people who get sick suffer with altitude sickness and either take medicine or get to lower altitude to recover. In comparison to climbing to the peak of Mount Everest it is extremely safe.

The danger really begins at higher altitude due to the more adverse weather conditions, limited oxygen and greater risk of fatal falls. Despite this, Everest Base Camp still carries some severe risks due to its location and altitude. The devastating earthquake that struck Nepal on the 25th of April 2015 was a strong reminder of just how vulnerable the base camp is to avalanches, claiming the lives of nineteen climbers and becoming the deadliest disaster on the mountain.

After some valuable time with Priyanka and Kunal, three snow-covered lads from Adelaide, Australia arrived back from their acclimatisation hike and looked completely dead. The Aussie group crashed, lying down and all holding their heads complaining that they felt dizzy.

That was the acclimatisation hike that I should have been doing, but instead, as ever, I tried to be a smart arse. It was another big wake-up call seeing them like that. God knows what state I would have been in if I had carried on to Lobuche without the extra acclimatisation day.

I had still not seen any of the people I had previously met. The guesthouses are so spread out. I kept meeting people on the trek and saying "see you there" but would never see them again. I presumed Takashi had made his way back down as he was running out of days on his trip and Jasmine must have been a day ahead of me.

I decided to spend 600 rupees on Wi-Fi after three days without it. I was dreading the endless amount of needy, worried-sick messages I would receive from Mum when I reconnected my phone.

I didn't even get one message. I mean, one would have been nice. Thanks Mum.

At this point of the trip, I was using socks for gloves as I stupidly lost my gloves. I would genuinely be fucked without Frosty lending me the rest of the gear. I would have spent a lot of money and no doubt would have bought the wrong clothing.

The past twelve hours had been a real mental and physical battle – vertigo, anxiety, disjointed breathing, panic and the freezing temperatures. It continued into the night. I kept waking up in panic, gasping for air. I'm not sure if they were night terrors or what. Either way, got no fucking sleep.

Staring at the wall to pass the time thoughts:

- *Will tomorrow be any better?*

I realised this was the first time on the trip that any doubt had set in. I had never experienced a climate this extreme before, my body just simply was not used to it. I didn't know if it was going to be any better the following day. Maybe it was my issues with asthma as a kid coming back to haunt me. I started to consider that maybe there was nothing I could do about it and like many others before me, I would have to make the trip back down without reaching the promised land.

- *Take it even slower*

Maybe I had been getting ahead of myself and there was an element of competitiveness subconsciously pushing me to walk too fast. Eventually I would have to recognise that as long as I get there it doesn't matter how long it takes.

- *Should I ditch the boots that are currently tied to the bottom of my bag?*

By this point, I was absolutely sick to death of carrying the heavy boots that were given to me, which were repeatedly swinging back and booting me up the arse with every step. I was concerned about getting blisters with the new boots, so I decided to make the executive decision and continue to trek in the Nike trainers.

If I ditched them, my work colleague probably would have been pissed, but all I could think about was the relief it would give me on my back.

Oh, and my red arse. Not felt pain like this since 'Arse Whacks' in the school playground. For the kids who spent their lunch times in the library, we used to play a game called 'Heads and Volleys' using a football. The loser got pinned against a fence, had to pull their pants down and have 30-40 lads line up, one by one and smash a football against their bare cheeks. Welcome to England.

Thinking back, I could have donated them which might have softened the blow of some expensive, Antarctic hiking boots being unreturned. Although, I did look around and no one seemed to have size 12 feet there.

DINGBOCHE (4410m) to LOBUCHE (4940m) – SECOND ATTEMPT

Slow and Steady

TRAVEL TIP: *"Go at a bloody slow pace, AT ALL TIMES"* is the advice.

What a difference meeting the three lads from Adelaide made. I got talking to Adrian, Matt and Darren and they were happy for me to tag along and join their group for the day - for the second attempt up to Lobuche. I realised just how fast I had previously been walking. Maybe I was getting accustomed to Ngima's speed. They kept a slow, steady pace from the off, staying together in a line, the guide at the front, the three lads in single-file behind and the porter at the back. Even in the flat areas, they were taking baby steps.

From here on I didn't have any more problems. Online, they advise only to have Diamox when you're actually sick. I took two halves of a pill throughout the journey in the hope it would block any potential or further sickness.

The Adelaide Convoy

Scott Fischer's memorial stone

Please don't look to me for pharmaceutical advice, I'm just telling you what I did. You need to ask a doctor or pharmacist.

Up to lunch, it was a fairly steady climb. After however, looked like the wall from Game of Thrones, a steep climb that looked near on vertical. At the top, there was a memorial for fallen climbers. No one really spoke when we arrived there; everyone took their time to look around and take it all in and the realisation of where we were and the dangers surrounding us set in.

I spotted a stone laid for Scott Fischer. He was admired by the mountaineering community for taking on the world's highest mountains without the use of supplemental oxygen. With his company *Mountain Madness*, Scott led a group of 18 people in climbing Mount Everest, but on May 11th 1996 he died after being caught in a blizzard and falling ill. He reached the summit on May 10th after 3:45pm - much later than the safe turnaround time of 2:00pm. This was due to the unusually high number of climbers who tried to make it to the summit on the same day. Jake Glynehall played Scott Fischer in the 2015 film *Everest*.

From *Game of Thrones* to *Lord of the Rings*. The next passage was comparable to Mordor, a grey rocky terrain, which was fairly flat but went on for miles.

Upon arrival at Lobuche, I unpacked my things into my new bedroom and checked my pockets… "Twat!" I had taken the room key from my lodge in Dingboche. Ngima wasn't best pleased as he now had to work out a way of returning it.

Final stretch to Lobuche   **Arriving in Lobuche**

When I went to take a seat for dinner, there were barely any tables left. All the sherpas in Lobuche must have gathered together to play this intense game of cards. They were all really animated, laughing and shouting across the table, which was incredibly amusing to watch.

I took up a small table beside them and as I sat down, I heard a strong Sydney accent say "Hey".

It was Jasmine, who I had not seen since leaving Namche. It turned out we had a lot in common. Both of us were trekking alone, currently living in Sydney, studied film and upload semi-decent travel photos to Instagram.

We had some food and chatted for a few hours, discussing our past travel stories and similarities. Later in the evening we joined Taylor from the Isle of White, and Paul from the United States, who were travelling together and we played cards till it was time to hit the hay.

It was coming to the end of the journey up to Everest Base Camp and it was nice to spend some time with Jasmine, Taylor and Paul. It was almost like a mini celebration as we were so close and we got to reflect over the past few days leading up to Lobuche.

One more *sleeping-bag-less* night's sleep and then I would arrive at Everest Base Camp!

Lobuche Prices (In Nepalese Rupee):

Macaroni Cheese = 650
Bottle of Water = 400
Bottle of Coca Cola = 470
Toilet Roll = 500

LOBUCHE (4940m) to EVEREST BASE CAMP (5365m) TO GORAKSEP (5165m)
A Life-Long Dream

I woke up feeling fresh for the first time. I managed to get a good eight hours - most probably down to exhaustion as my muscles were aching from days of uphill walking with a heavy weight on my back. It was a nice change to the past few nights where I was waking up in my sleep every five minutes gasping for air.

The last village before EBC was Goraksep, where we would stay the night. It's around halfway from Lobuche to EBC and this is where we would stop to check in and drop any baggage we wouldn't need for the day. It was a long gradual incline through a rocky valley and the views were breath-taking. Quite literally.

The walk up to Goraksep

As we walked adjacent to the Khumbu glacier you could hear the crackle of some small avalanches to your right. I think that startled a few people, but for me that just added to the excitement. I treated it more as a drum roll. You could now really start to feel the shortage of breath as we surpassed the 5000 metre mark. The oxygen at this altitude is 50% to that of sea level. I noticed I was taking quicker and deeper breaths to accommodate the lack of oxygen, but I kept reminding myself to walk slowly and remain calm. It is natural for the body to start breathing like this to allow more fresh oxygen into the lungs.

Goraksep – last stop before EBC

I woz ere, Goraksep lodge

I took a seat beside Jasmine while we waited for our guides to check us in. We noticed names hand written all over the walls of people who had passed through this lodge, so I decided to add mine. As I finished the 'd' on McLeod, she gasped. Her mother's family name was McLeod, also spelt exactly the same. Even more things in common. The small world gets smaller.

The beginning of the hike from Goraksep involved trudging through thick mud, which I hadn't experienced anywhere else. After about a mile of mud, it became much rockier to the point where we were climbing over huge boulders. People kept telling me this was the hardest stretch they had experienced, but I think I was just riding a wave of high morale and adrenalin that I didn't find it tough at all. I was just so determined to make it to Base Camp and tick off a huge dream of mine.

Having Orbital and Leftfield in my ear did help though. Orbital and Leftfield are two electronic dance music duos who my dad got me in to and the pumping rave music had been the perfect soundtrack to assist me in marching up the mountain.

Amazing view of the Himalayas

En route I bumped into 'Canadian Mike'. He'd just left Base Camp and said he and his girlfriend were getting a helicopter down. He claimed they had a headache. You can read into it what you will. We'll call them 'opportunists'.

One of the guides told me that some of the tourists take advantage of the insurance and pretend to have altitude sickness in order to secure a quick journey down. Have you really completed it if you don't walk... or run back down though?

Rescue helicopter leaving EBC   **First clear view of Base Camp**

After a tormenting succession of teasing corners, we finally saw the valley open out, revealing the stunning Khumbu Glacier and snow-capped Base Camp. It was a pretty special feeling.

It turned out to be a great decision to turn back and take an extra acclimatisation day in Dingboche, because as I arrived into the base camp, the weather was glorious! It was sunny, with crisp blue skies and I tried to spend as much time taking in the moment, but this was definitely a good time if ever to take some photos.

**Blue skies at Everest
Base Camp**   **Icy EBC**

I'll always, sort of remember the quote from my mate Eddie Robb, founder of the company *Make It Social*. He said, "Don't take so many photos that you don't actually live the moment." Something like that.

I felt so lucky to be there, at the foot of Mount Everest, the gateway to the top of the world. Something that I had dreamed about for so many years finally became a reality. Just looking around was giving me chills - and not just from the brisk winds. I tried to cover the whole camp by foot ensuring that I had seen every corner and every angle of it before leaving.

I had promised my work colleagues in Sydney at Watsons Bay Boutique Hotel that I would get a photo wearing the company jumper when I arrived at Base Camp. I fulfilled that promise and got a few other photos and videos for friends and family back home. Jasmine joined me for a photo on one of the larger rocks that sits in the middle of the camp. The rock was decorated in the local prayer flags and the flags of all the countries that have been represented at Base Camp in the past.

Watsons Bay jumper

**Jasmine, some flags
and I**

Vai Brasil!!!!!

The prayer flags are visible at many points throughout the journey, either draped in the local villages or tied to sacred buildings. The brightly coloured prayer flags - which have become iconic on the Everest Base Camp trek - consist of five colours – *blue* for the sky, *white* for the air/wind, *red* for fire, *green* for water and *yellow* for the earth. Different prayers and mantras on the flag are used to promote peace, compassion, strength and wisdom. Locals believe that when the wind blows the flags, it spreads the blessings and good will represented in the writings.

Prayer flags decorate Base Camp   **High quality mountaineering tents**

As you walk around Base Camp it's like a mini pop-up city with all the different travel and expedition companies dotted around in different tents. We were informed by one of the guides that there were more than three hundred people left to summit in the next few weeks. This was the final batch of mountaineers looking to test their fate against Everest this season. The majority of their time isn't actually spent climbing; it's spent planning, resting and acclimatising. There are two main base camps at the foot of Mount Everest, one on the Nepal side and one on the Tibet side.

Everest Base Camp sits at around 5365 metres. The reason it's not any higher is because it is simply not sustainable to live at any higher altitude for a prolonged period of time. At extreme altitude, your brain and lungs are starved for oxygen and the risk of having a heart attack is also increased.

Every year, more and more people are making their way to Base Camp to attempt the summit, making it incredibly dangerous. There are too many people, many of which are inexperienced climbers and this causes traffic jams up the mountain which can be fatal.

The sunshine and clear blue skies soon turned to blizzard. It's crazy how quickly the weather turns up there. It was cool to see Everest Base Camp in glorious sunshine as well as seeing it in the snowy conditions though. I tried to savour the moment for as long as possible. It was such an amazing feeling and sense of achievement, but I had to start making my way back as the storm was getting dangerously worse.

Storm brewing at EBC

During the spring, the temperature at Everest Base Camp can reach as high as 20 degrees Celsius in the day time. At night is a different story, the temperature can be as low as -15 degrees Celsius.

On my descent, shaking my head in awe and disbelief at the whole thing, I bumped into the Adelaide lads. We exchanged contacts in the hope we'd be able to meet up in Australia when I headed back there. They saved my trip in a sense, with their advice of "Slow and steady. Slow and steady".

Throughout the journey back, the snow was getting more and more intense and was starting to set. After around two hours of plodding through the snow I finally made it back to

Goraksep, and by this point the snow was now ankle-deep. I felt bad for the guys still at Base Camp as it would take them around three or four hours to get back fighting through that weather.

Without doubt these were the roughest bedrooms on the trip, but I was completely wiped out when I got back. I managed to get a few hours' nap before being woken up to hear someone banging on the door. It had been none-stop snow for the past four or five hours but somehow the clouds had cleared, which meant it was perfect weather for a sunset view of Everest. Ngima was going wild saying "we have to climb Kala Patthar."

Here I was, exhausted, getting some well-deserved rest and I was being woken up to the news that I have to climb another mountain, and it's three hundred metres higher than EBC!

We raced up Kala Patthar. Well, halfway up Kala Patthar. I was fucked. I couldn't go on. Halfway was enough for me, I just didn't have it in me, and we were going up far too fast. I could barely breathe, but I was breathless anyway from what I saw. Kala Patthar, meaning 'black rock' is, I guess, a kind of big hill, located on the south ridge of Pumori above Goraksep. Although it is not officially regarded as a mountain, the ascent of Kala Patthar is extremely popular within the trekking community as it provides a stunning view of Everest and is the only real close-up viewpoint that is accessible.

I don't feel comfortable saying the word magical, but it was magical. In fact, it was bloody marvellous. Of all the peaks on display, the sun was only shining on the Everest peak. Couldn't write it.

So, I typed it instead.

73

It was a fairy-tale ending. Apart from the fact that I had to now get down from this obscene height.

Sun only shining on Everest peak

Magical ending

Goraksep Prices (In Nepalese Rupee):

Pizza = 700
Bottle of Water = 400
Bottle of Coke = 450
Black Tea = 110

GORAKSEP (5165m) TO NAMCHE BAZAAR (3440m)

Run, Forrest. Run!

The news was starting to come through, confirming that flights were being delayed by up to three or four days. We were coming to the back end of the season and the weather was now starting to affect treks and flights. Missing my flight meant missing the wedding. Missing the wedding meant an angry mother.

Ngima and I discussed the situation, and we just about convinced ourselves that it was possible to cut the four days back to Lukla, down to two and try and book on to an earlier flight. Ngima told me that he once got back to Lukla in one day - a full day of running, but without any bags or anything weighing him down.

As we left at 6 am, there was an old Italian guy looking really worse for wear waiting for medical assistance. He looked as pale as a ghost, wrapped head to toe in warm clothing and blankets, with what looked to be his best mate with his arm around him. Once a rescue helicopter arrived to get him down the mountain, we set off on our way.

It's just something you have to learn to accept seeing things like that. Whilst people look out for each other, everyone puts themselves in this situation knowing the risk.

This was potentially the hardest day and it was all downhill. 50km across the Himalayas back to Namche Bazaar with a heavy AF backpack and dangling boots that I never even used, bashing the back of my legs with every movement. I will never know how I did it. I'd not exercised for seven months.

About two hours in I bumped into Taylor who we'd been playing cards with the previous night. He told us he woke up with severe altitude sickness and a pain that was like a never-ending drill in his head, so he had to leave in the middle of the night and walk down to Lobuche wearing a head torch. You know it's bad when getting up in the middle of the night in minus temperatures, in complete darkness just to get to lower altitude is the only option. His trekking group only consisted of two people so they had to split up. He took the guide and Paul stayed with the porter.

We ran through Pangboche, which is around the halfway mark between Dingboche and Tengboche, and sits at 3985 metres. It's a small, scenic village with an old monastery nestled in the middle of the valley, surrounded by spectacular views on either side. Pangboche used to be one of the busiest villages until tourism created the need for lodges to be built closer to Mount Everest.

Beware, Pangboche

Golden Rules of Altitude

It is common to see warnings and reminders at many of the restaurants and lodges to ensure you look after yourself at high altitude. The staff and locals are always on hand with the relevant advice and experience to assist you if you are in trouble. At the *Everest Kitchen* they used a poster with their 'Golden Rules of Altitude'. This included reminders that if you feel unwell; you probably have altitude sickness, you should descend immediately and you need to drink plenty of fluids.

As we walked past a school, we noticed two children arguing at the bottom of the steps. The younger brother was crying and refusing to hold the older brother's hand. I had a degree of sympathy seeing as they have to climb 500 metres just to go to school. I would've had a right tantrum at that age, bless him.

Refusing to go to school

Gateway to Everest from Tengboche

On the steep downhill from Tengboche to the *river-village-place* where I'd stopped at previously for lunch, I decided to make use of the sharp descent. This consisted of thirty minutes of me sprinting/falling down the mountain. My guide couldn't keep up, telling me that he had never had a client go so fast, especially with a backpack. God knows what all the people struggling uphill were thinking as I came flying past. I'm sure they would laugh if they knew I was late for a wedding.

I remember the days of watching people with big grins on their face passing you by downhill, carefree as you sweated it up the mountain, and just thinking to yourself...

"Twat".

"Twat".

"Twat."

"Hi, yeah good thanks, not."

"Twat."

My knees really hurt when I got down to the bottom – obviously. I had never run that fast in my life. I felt like Usain Bolt, without the bolt. The guides and porters would ask me where I had come from. When I told them I had travelled from Goraksep, they wouldn't believe me.

This way to Namche Bazaar

For the final stretch to Namche it was just going on and on and up and up. Every corner looked like the end and it never was. It was torture and the conditions were getting worse with the falling temperatures. I was seriously craving a radiator and a *qualm-free zone* like a film in bed with a bag of strawberry laces. You can get three for a quid in the Co-op. Check it out, it's insane.

The only thing keeping me pressing onward was the thought of a beer at the Irish bar. It was in my sights. I felt like *Harold and Kumar* trying to get to the *White Castle*.

When I finally reached and collapsed at the lodge, my legs were shaking. It was easily the most tired I've ever been. It reminded me of the time when my dad participated in the Santiago marathon in Chile. As well as it being a red-hot day, it was below oxygen safety levels, due to pollution in the city. He suffered from such severe muscle spasms that he ended up in the back of an ambulance.

My body was just zapped of everything. No energy, no morale... no sleeping bag. I actually thought about buying a sleeping bag now that I was back in Namche with some money, just for a laugh. I could finally get a warm night's sleep in before I flew out. This was obviously a stupid idea, to add to all my other stupid ideas, so I went for a pint - the one I had envisioned in my mind, the one that had kept me going all that way. It was magnificent. I don't have enough superlatives to describe how good that pint tasted.

Timings:

7:00 am - Set off from Goraksep
8:00 am – Arrived at Lobuche
8:45 am – Descended the 'Wall of Death'
9:30 am – Arrived at Pheriche
10:30 am – Arrived at Pangboche
12:45 pm – Arrived at Tengboche
1:30 pm - Arrived at the *river-village-place*
4:00 pm – Arrived at Namche Bazaar

NAMCHE BAZAAR (3440m) to LUKLA (2860m)

Nepali Belly

I woke up feeling great. Yeah, my legs were in bits, but today's journey would be nothing compared to yesterday. It would be mainly all downhill to Lukla and not nearly as far. I was nearly there. I just had to hope that I could change my flight to one leaving in the morning; otherwise I had run for nothing. And that would be really fucking devastating. In fact, if that happened, I don't think I'd ever run again.

Despite not going as mental as the day before, I still managed to make it to Lukla in good time. I ran down the steep parts, but limited myself to walking on the flat areas. It was amusing recognising certain spots along the way, getting flashbacks of the numerous times I was struggling up the hill. "Oh, that's the stone I sat on when I couldn't breathe," "Oh that's where I tripped over a step," "Oh that's where I thought we were nearly in Namche, but we were actually still three hours away."

The stretch between Namche and Lukla was one of the most scenic and memorable parts of the trip. The narrow, overshadowed path winds its way through the forest, but when there is a break in the trees, you are rewarded with some of the most extraordinary mountain scenery in Nepal.

As I arrived back into Lukla I met a girl called Ola, who worked for the Canadian Red Bull. She was travelling with her father and writing a blog about her experiences. He was a bit further behind because he'd been dealing with varying degrees of sickness throughout the trip. Once he had caught up to us, I said hello and we agreed to meet up later on in the evening for a drink.

Arriving back at the lodge and putting my feet up allowed me some time to reflect. I was immensely proud of what I had achieved and there was a real sense of satisfaction knowing that I had pulled it off with no planning, training or any real prior experience.

The worn-out feet, tight muscles and sore joints were merely a hindrance as I flicked through the photos from the trip, appreciating how bloody outstanding it has been.

Nepal had without doubt cemented itself as my favourite country to date. The views were out of this world and the people were so friendly and accommodating. I've never been to a country where I have felt so welcome by the local people.

I can't recommend this country and the Everest Base Camp trek enough. It was a life changing experience and it's everything I was hoping it would be and more. As well as the obvious physical aspect, it was a really tough challenge mentally. I was constantly having to gear myself up to keep going, but the battle made it all the more sweet when I made it to the end.

I'm many years of training and many thousands of dollars away, but who knows... maybe a seed has been planted to come back and attempt the summit one day.

After all the spices, dahl's and street food I'd somehow managed to survive *Nepali Belly* up until now. This all changed after an absolute nightmare at Ngima's family house. They cooked a lovely meal for me, but unfortunately as soon as I got into bed, my stomach started churning.

I can't go into details, but picture Harry in *Dumb and Dumber* after Lloyd dropped laxatives in his drink. Now picture this whilst being stuck in an outside toilet in subzero temperatures with no toilet roll, no clothes and no light.

If you want, I can go into more details because it was fucking hilarious and was like something out of a film.

I'll save it for another time.

Safe to say I didn't leave the house that night.

LUKLA (2860m) to KATHMANDU (1400m)

Ngima – The Hero

It was basically a game of chance when we arrived at the airport. One, because I didn't know if I could even get on an earlier flight and two, I didn't know if I'd even make it to Kathmandu without the plane crashing. The weather was looking really temperamental.

How it works is, there are four airlines, and two planes per airline. Each plane does two trips (This isn't a riddle or a maths GCSE question by the way). So, there are four trips with the same airline per day, which means four opportunities for me to go. I had to fly with the same airline I had originally booked with, if I was to change my flight. I made my way to the airport for the first flight. Ngima tried working his magic by speaking to different people he knew

Scenic view from Lukla Airport **Dangerously cool airport**

but they couldn't get me on, the flight was fully booked.

An hour or so later I tried again, loitering around the airline desk trying to find a way, but again there was no luck. This was really deflating because I'd been really optimistic, anticipating to be in Kathmandu before it was midday. As I left to go back, I saw a man walking up the steps of the plane I had hoped to be on, fist pumping the air to comical effect. I laughed and then realised it was Kunal who I had met in Dingboche. Who else?

Ngima was an absolute hero. He told me to chill at his mother in law's home, whilst he stayed at the airport to try and pull strings. He said he would ring me if he got the go ahead. After two hours or so, I was starting to lose hope and accept the fact that I would have to stay another night.

Until the phone rang.

I was still a bit dubious, but I rushed over to the airport for the third time and Ngima had actually, somehow managed to get me onto the next flight. To make things even more incredible Ola was at the check-in desk and catching the same flight. I gave Ngima some skin and a hug and I promised him that we would see each other again. We'd been through a lot. Well, he'd been through a lot looking after me, so I was fully determined to make that reunion happen.

I sat with Ola and her dad while we waited for our flight. Ola's dad was worried that he might have pneumonia. I didn't really get it. Normally kids really worry about their parents but she was more like "Dad, man up. It's just a sore throat" which I found quite funny.

The plane was even smaller than last time and had half the number of seats. The turbulence was non-existent; however, I'd say it was worse because we were flying through thick cloud the whole way. You couldn't see anything. You couldn't see planes coming the other way, couldn't see the cliff faces... Ola asked if I was a nervous flyer - of course I said no, but I was feeling this one a little.

Return to Normality, Sort Of

Arriving back in Kathmandu was amazing; there was a sense of relief as I had made it back in one piece, there was a bit of normality by being back in a big city and I could finally have my first hot shower in nearly two weeks. I must have stood in there for about twenty minutes. With there being no possibility of Ngima banging on the door asking me to climb any more mountains, I went to take some kip.

After a few hours of bliss, I woke up to find some messages from Kunal and Priyanka, who as ever were full of energy – evident in the string of messages demanding me to come out. Their joyful sense of humour saved me in Dingboche, so I felt obliged to return the favour. After watching the Liverpool game on my own, I joined them for dinner. Dinner turned into shots. Shots turned into bar crawl. Bar crawl turned into thinking I can dance like Fred Astaire.

It's not quite Ibiza, but you aren't short of exciting bars and clubs in the centre of Thamel. I really liked how the locals and tourists were dancing, drinking and celebrating together, creating the perfect vibe to wind down after the arduous trek. There are casinos in Kathmandu if you're that way inclined, but I'd been gambling enough, (with my life) so I passed up on the opportunity.

I'd met many interesting, like-minded people throughout the trip and was eager to stay in touch and meet up with them again in the future. Although temporary, it was fun to be a part of the trekking community. Everyone I met was incredibly friendly and I really valued the conversations and time I spent with them.

There was time for a hungover day walking around Thamel, souvenir shopping, and packing all my belongings together. I wouldn't say I'm a collector but I try and get a t-shirt from every place I've been, so I picked up a few more Everest Base Camp t-shirts and got a couple of presents for my parents. In the day time Thamel is a great place for shopping. You can buy spices, teas, incense, jewellery and it's also really famous for traditional Nepalese paintings and clothing – most notably pashmina. The plan was to get the plane out of Nepal the next morning. Obviously, it didn't go as smoothly as I was hoping.

Remarkably, I had arrived back to Kathmandu even earlier than planned, so my lovely mother managed to change my international flight to a day earlier so I wasn't rushing so much getting to the wedding. When I arrived at the airport, they made it as difficult as humanly possible. Because she had used her card to pay the fee for the flight change, they required a photocopy of her card, signature and ID.

Bearing in mind it was 2 o'clock in the morning back home and my mum was asleep, this was a massive ball ache. Not to mention I was running out of time before the check-in desks closed. I also didn't have a phone that could make calls in Nepal, so I had to get the Wi-Fi password.

For some reason, the Wi-Fi only worked behind the check-in desks, so I had to stand there and I just started messaging any random person who was online on Facebook, asking them to ring my mum's mobile. Knowing my mum, it was probably downstairs or on silent. As well as sending her messages, I tried ringing her on WhatsApp and

Facebook in the hope that it would make her phone beep. This went on for over an hour.

Then I remembered house phones still existed. I asked my friend Jay, in Scotland, to call my house phone. He wasn't too keen on waking my mum up in the middle night, but if he didn't, I'd be staying in Nepal and missing my flight.

He explained the situation and she sent over the documents. Once I received them, I then had to send them to their head office. Eventually they were accepted and I was given the green light.

This was until they noticed my drone. They tried their best making an issue out of me using it as hand luggage. The guy at the desk was calling a few people asking for second opinions. I kept insisting that it was legal, that I fly with it everywhere, and eventually they gave up and let me on the plane.

I'm probably one of the most unprepared and unorganised people to ever complete the Everest Base Camp trek, but I did it.

And against all odds, I made it to the wedding.

Katie and Paul's wedding

ACKNOWLEDGEMENTS

The irony is, this all started by me just writing a few things down about my experiences each day to keep me busy, as I didn't have a book to read *(Staring at the wall to pass the time thoughts)*. At that point I didn't even know if it would go far enough to be a blog, never mind a book. When I got back home, I decided it was a story worth telling in blog format, so I made a website and posted it in eight parts online. People seemed to enjoy the story, so I made the decision to develop it into a book some time later. I couldn't have done it without the help of a few people though.

Firstly, I would like to thank Ngima for getting me home in one piece. He may be a fast walker, but he's a great guy and really gave me the best advice to keep me safe when I most needed it. I hope I can get back to Nepal in the near future so we can catch up.

Thanks to my parents, Karen and Ian for putting up with my adventures and apologies for putting you through all the stress. Although, it is your fault I have a passion for travelling.

Huge thanks to Gwenda Thomas and Dave Hall for being fantastic help on the editing front and making sure everything was in order and made sense. I think the editing took longer than the actual writing of the book.

Thank you to David Ayre who has been incredible in showing me the ropes with publishing my first book and giving me invaluable advice along the way.

Thank you to Manda, Kate and Lauren who got me on my feet in Australia and looked after me before I headed to

Nepal and thanks to the Manning Road family for supporting my idea to go to Everest with two days' notice. Thank you also to Kylie, my good friend and manager for letting me leave my job for Nepal at short notice and helping me to find work when I returned to Sydney.

Big thanks to Kelly, Ryan, Emma and Rich for housing and feeding me for the several weeks I spent at theirs finishing off the book. I hope all the washing up I did was enough to cover my rent!

And cheers to my mates in Harrogate and Dubai for not disowning me yet. I know you were sick of me talking about the book and asking for advice. Every time we met, I was becoming the butt end of every joke, like that scene in Family Guy with Brian and Stewie. "Look at the bright side; you have some new material for that novel you've been writing. You know...the novel you've been workin' on? You know the, the one, uh, you've been workin on for three years? You know the novel. Got somethin' new to write about now. You know?"

Finally, thank you to everyone who has given their support to the book and taken time aside to read it. I've really enjoyed the writing experience and I have so many more travel stories to tell, so I'm hoping to follow this up with a few more books in the next year. I'm also working on a travel screenplay for a feature length film, so fingers crossed I can get that finished in the near future.

Get in touch and tag me with a photo of you and your copy of the book at:

Instagram - @clodblog
Twitter - @clodblog1

Thanks again,

Cory

Printed in Great Britain
by Amazon